My Spirit Flies

Portraits and Prose
of
Women In Their Power

My Spirit Flies

Portraits and Prose
of
Women In Their Power

M. Cathy Angell

Bay City Press

Bellingham, Washington

My Spirit Flies: Portraits and Prose of Women In Their Power

Copyright © 1997 by M. Cathy Angell
All rights reserved.

ISBN 0-9655459-3-8

Library of Congress Catalog Card Number: 96-95260

Bay City Press - Box 1213 - Bellingham, WA 98227 - USA - (360) 714-1982

Book Design & Layout: Lanphear Design
Printed in the United States of America by Walsworth Publishing Company

*Dedicated to the memory of
my Aunt Chrystal Finley,
a strong and elegant woman
who lived with dignity and grace.*

Foreword

Picture a woman doing what she loves, being fully present, experiencing her own power. It is as if her whole life journey has propelled her, like a shooting star, to this one awesome and ordinary moment. What does that look like? We have all seen her, everywhere, but have we ever really paused to consider her? She is beautiful in her self-contained power.

In our daily lives, out in the world, and in our homes, we experience such women. We might take what we experience for granted. This book invites us to take another look. These women are strong and vibrant in their feminine power. They aren't trying to be pretty, or trying to be powerful like a man. In fact, they aren't "trying" at all. They simply are. Being women.

In Western patriarchal society, we have been brought up on "Barbie Doll" images of what a woman should look like and fed television models of her absurd behavior. In the advertisements we are bombarded with every day, we have become brainwashed about the beauty of women, forgetting to acknowledge the many other options. What is beauty? What is strength of character, and power? Today's woman is quite extraordinary because she is really coming into her own in terms of her feminine strengths. Although many women may still be trying to be that face in the magazine, many others are not. Many are exploring what it is to be free. Free to be Herself, in her fullest expression.

Through her photography, Cathy Angell helps us to witness the expansiveness of what it means to be a powerful woman. Depth of character and spirit shine through each portrait. The photographs show different aspects of "a woman in her power" as if she were a many-faceted gem, where an expanse of age and skin tone are part of what makes her priceless. Beauty doesn't come from a certain kind of mascara, or style of clothing, but from the center of a woman who knows who she is. *My Spirit Flies* shifts the image of women to a healthier place.

As you look through these pages, you automatically begin to search for someone you know. We all have friends, mothers, sisters, or even an image of ourselves that we can imagine included here. Viewing the portraits may help us to honor the powerful women in our own lives and, perhaps, listen to what they have to say. You can see in their faces that they have stories to tell. They have all taken risks to be who they are. It is not the easy path to break out of the "Barbie Doll" wanna-be mold. To be seen as they stand in their truth is their victory.

It is very comforting and exciting to know that the women portrayed in this book are real. They aren't acting out a part for this publication but are living in their power daily. Let us acknowledge that all women are beautiful in their power stance and appreciate their unique versions of strength in the feminine spirit.

Thank you, women, for living your truth, which is where your power lies.

How would your world be different, if you had grown up in a house that had this book on the coffee table?

Walk in beauty,
Starfeather

(Starfeather is an artist and writer who facilitates women's circles and spiritual retreats in the Pacific Northwest.)

The Power Project

*F*ive years ago, an idea grabbed me and did not let go: to photograph women in their power and create a traveling exhibit. The women I mentioned it to responded with a resounding "YES! Do this!" It felt like a calling....and scared me to death.

For the next four years, I made mental and emotional preparations. I increased my knowledge of black and white photography. I wrote down goals. I talked about the idea with many different women. *And* I kept placing obstacles in my path. I would start the project after I learned more. After I bought a better camera. After I purchased a computer. After I healed from the break-up of a long-term relationship. After I was accepted into a graduate program and could do it as a thesis project. *It's amazing how effectively we can block ourselves from doing those things which feel so right.* I finally started the project after I made some honest decisions in other areas of my life. I left a job that wasn't working for me. I turned down the offer to go to graduate school. I moved out of the city to a town where I had wanted to live for a long time. I had a wonderful partner. Finally, with no more excuses, I had to start. So I stepped into my power....

Almost immediately, the energy and momentum started building, and the project took off. I felt passionately focused. I started living life with ease, rather than struggle. I felt more present and less distracted. I felt vitalized and full and happy. I was *living* in my power.

Over the months, the project evolved to include a book. The number of participants increased. Personal essays were added. I made a conscious decision to just let it flow and, subsequently, learned some big lessons about how things move smoothly when you are living in your passion and coming from your heart.

Often, when I started talking with a woman about my project, she quickly ruled herself out. She suggested instead someone well-known or famous. But *she* was actually the type of woman I wanted to have in the book. *Every woman is powerful, regardless of her credentials.* For this reason, I chose to downplay information that we often use to label and separate ourselves from other people, such as job titles, academic degrees, and career successes.

The process of working with each woman involved several steps. The first step was to help her explore those times when she felt passionate, strong, focused, creative, and balanced. She identified those times when she felt good about herself, loved what she was doing and was coming from a place of truth. Almost without fail, the participant couldn't positively identify her place of power before, first, going through this exercise. As women, we aren't used to thinking about ourselves as being powerful. We tend to minimize those times in our lives, thinking that they aren't significant or important enough.

The next step was to develop a photographic concept. This came after the participant had listed all of the times when she felt in her power and allowed one particular time to rise above the others. I would ask her what that image looked like in her mind, and she would describe it. This part of the process was always suspenseful for me because I rarely knew where we were going to end up. But whatever she said, I went along with it. Of course, sometimes her answer caused me to stretch a bit, especially when it involved doing backwards loops in a plane or climbing up the steep face of a cliff!

But every experience was a treat, no matter how challenging. It was a gift to be involved with each woman in such a personal way. To see and share a special slice of her life. And it was always such a high for me during the shoot to see that moment when she shifted into her power. That moment when she dropped self-consciousness and became engaged and involved in whatever she was doing. That was the moment I wanted to capture. And it always happened. When a woman is doing something she loves, she can't help but be drawn into that place of passion and focus.

The final part of the process involved asking the participants to edit the words they spoke during the intake interview. In her own unique way, each woman developed a paragraph that explained the meaning of her portrait.

As these were being completed, the idea to include essays was born. The essays were written by women who identified their inner power and wrote about their experiences. Their words add depth and insight to the personal process that each woman went through to be a part of this book.

Some general reactions that were initially prevalent for most of the women were: Am I really powerful? What am I doing when I'm in my power? I'm nervous. I don't know what to say. What if I can't come up with anything? ...And then they settled down, and settled in, and shifted their vision. *Then they could see what everyone else sees.* It was a beautiful thing.

M. Cathy Angell

Portraits and Prose

Mother Love

My baby has changed my life. I no longer have to ask myself who I am or how I fit in. I am a mother. This has allowed me to step into my full self: protector, nurturer, teacher, provider and student.

I love how my body makes nourishment. I love giving my baby a bath, watching him sleep, and playing with him. I am in awe of his growth and transformation from a newborn to a little person.

I'm most in my power when I let my capacity for loving reach beyond the boundaries.

Felicia Soth
Age 23

As a little girl growing up, one of the earliest places I found for being in my power was through basketball. Without even realizing it, a simple game nurtured convictions of dedication, teamwork, commitment, honesty and respect for others. A simple game became a conduit for self-confidence.

One of my favorite commercials depicts various little girls at play, and the accompanying words say something to the effect: "Everyday in America a little girl is born...and someone will tell her she is beautiful, and someone will tell her she is strong, and someone will tell her she is precious, and someone will tell her she is tough...and someone will give her a doll, and then someone will give her a ball...and then someone will give her a chance."

There can be special moments in a game when you forget everything else around you. Nothing else exists but you, an intensity, a focus and a simple joy about what you're doing. A pure, radiant, and powerful celebration of life itself.

Cheryl Bishop
Age 32

Trust Yourself to Believe

When I'm singing spirit songs, it feels like I've stepped aside to let the songs come through me. It usually happens when I'm connected with the earth - that's where the songs come from.

People like my singing, and it's powerful when my songs travel and go through their beings. That's when it strikes a chord. It is a sense of power knowing that it is good.

Today, I went searching
For God, Goddess, All That Is.
But all I found was
A field of tall green grass
And yellow iris at the water's edge,
Blooming in the sunlight.

Sandy Howard
Age 48

Singing With Spirit

At Home

*I'm in my power when I'm flying in a challenging mode -
turbulence, bad weather, isolated strips at night. Also when I'm
teaching someone who is excited about flying.*

*I've always had an affinity for testing my limits. I used to compete in
aerial acrobatic skiing where I'd do flips off snow jumps. Now I've taken
that aptitude into aerobatic flying. I feel comfortable, natural, and focused
as I do loops, spins, and rolls. I'm very present and there is no clutter in
my mind.*

Kerri Ballard
Age 37

Quest for the Unexplored

Research, whether fisheries or archeology, is like waking up on Christmas morning. You never know what strange creatures or objects may appear in the dredge or net or unearthed from the ground. It's rare to find new species. But the work involved to make those discoveries is necessary and rewarding in itself.

Life on the boat is not a luxurious experience. The challenges of working around Mother Nature are unending. Trying to obtain good scientific information in 20 foot seas is a struggle, especially in Alaska. On other days, the seas are calm and the scenery is picturesque. Often I am the only woman, but the mental and physical isolation give me time to reflect and relax from our fast-paced world.

When I'm out at sea, I am more in tune to the rhythms of our planet. It is the quest for the unexplored that continues to guide and push me further.

Teresa Turk
Age 35

Splitting Image

*T*ai Kwon Do has given me a sense of strength and self-esteem that I haven't felt before. It requires discipline and self-challenge to learn various forms of kicks, punches, and self-defense moves.

For more than two years I had thought about getting my black belt when I turned 62. A week after my birthday, I took the test. I had to break six consecutive boards barefooted with six different kicks. I also had to do a hand break, which I didn't think I could do. When it was time, you could have heard a pin drop. I hit the board with the palm of my hand, and it exploded. The audience erupted into the biggest cheer and applause I've ever had.

It's amazing what it does to your inner feeling when you have a success and there's someone watching. It's not just a physical accomplishment, it's an inner sense that I worked hard for this.

Nancy Parsley
Age 62

I have come to the realization that I want to do healing work at this juncture of my life. I'm being certified in acupuncture and working in a clinic. It is satisfactory work to be of service to people - especially women in need. It resonates with me spiritually because it is fulfilling and rewarding.

My ultimate goal is to help others feel better about themselves and to empower them through healing. People say that they totally trust what I am doing. I've created a non-threatening and safe place to be.

Rashida G. Harris
Age 47

Harmony Comes When It Flows in a Balanced Way

I Am a Mother

Not long ago I was with a group of women on retreat at the ocean. When Cathy Angell arrived, it reminded me that I had forgotten to follow up on having my photograph in her book. Later, she spoke to me and asked what had happened.

What *had* happened? It wasn't just a little "oops, I forgot" kind of a thing. It had been a big "completely gone from my mind, it never happened" kind of thing. I knew I needed to take a look.

Several months earlier I had asked to be included. I remembered well my yearning to have my picture be in her book...my longing to be seen as a "woman of power." When Cathy said yes and actually took me up on it, I became terrified. "Me? Oh my gosh! What could I possibly do that would be interesting enough - powerful enough - to be in a book? Am I out of my mind? I'm not a woman of power. I'm just a mom...a sometimes artist...a sometimes lots of things." You know the list. Stuff that women/mothers do all the time.

I care for my children. I tend the earth. I grow flowers. I write in my journal. I prepare food for my family. I read to my daughter. I give hugs and tender touches and smiles. Sometimes I frown...a lot. I draw and paint. I bead. I build fires. I clean. I pray. I sing. I listen. I yell. I work. I cry. I heal. I play my drum. I talk with friends. I feed the birds.

Stuff that women do all the time.

Not long ago I was giving information to a police officer. When he asked my occupation I said, "I'm a mother and an artist." He wrote down "artist," omitting mother altogether. So, being a mother often feels like invisible work. In fact, so commonplace, our culture doesn't even see it as work at all. I have no "job" and am therefore less than others...certainly not worthy of having my picture in a book about women in their power.

Now, looking over the description of all that I do, I see how big it is. Here on paper it suddenly seems more - much more - than the daily doing of it. I begin to see the truth. If women see themselves - if you or I see ourselves - as anything less than powerful, capable, creative beings, it is simply a lie.

The truth is that living my life *is* an act of power. Being a mother and all else that I do *is* powerful. It is time for each of us to honor who we are and acknowledge the gifts we give each day. The gifts of our time, our presence, our hearts. The gifts of intelligence, sensitivity, and strength. That afternoon at the beach, as Cathy and I talked, I saw that my disbelief in myself as worthy was something I most likely shared with many women. I thought writing of this would be valuable. Cathy agreed. And so, the idea of essays as part of her project was birthed.

My photograph is not on these pages. My words are.

I am standing in a place of power.

I invite you to join me.

-Vhey Benet
Age 44

Riverdancer

I feel the gift of life in its highest intensity while I am dancing. I am giving energy to others, to the Earth, to myself and to life. There is love flowing back and forth through all of these.

I love dancing to drums. Listening to them inspires movement and makes me feel connected to the Earth and Spirit. I can feel myself radiate when I dance and am filled with joy to see how my dancing touches others. It is the gift that Spirit has given me to express my truest self and contribute my light to the circle of life.

Marissa Baratian
Age 25

What Children Become Tomorrow, Depends on Us Today

My strongest passion is working with young children.

As director of a program that focuses on children with special needs and with my own background as a person with a disability, I have come to realize the importance of being able to communicate effectively. Many children have trouble interacting. It is important to be able to express oneself and to be able to understand others, regardless of how this is accomplished.

Our preschool program includes children with and without special needs who are from several ethnic backgrounds. I believe that the key to a stronger society is to realize that diversity enriches us. It does not tear us apart. If we don't influence children to see value in one another, we will face great difficulty in making our society a better place for all of us.

"A hundred years from now it will not matter what my bank account was, the sort of house I lived in, or the kind of car I drove...but the world may be a better place because I made a difference in the life of a child." -unknown

Joan Nourse Martin
Age 53

They Understand

Teaching can be a blast. Of course there is much that is mundane about it, and there are also many frustrations. But, sometimes, when I can feel the students are with me, there is nothing like it. This can happen when I have explained a statistical concept five different ways and, finally, after filling a wall of chalkboard or jumping around for half an hour physically demonstrating probability or linear regression, their faces brighten with understanding. Or we could be discussing an environmental issue, and I see that some of them are thinking about the environment or social justice in a way that has never occurred to them before. New questions emerge for them and their worlds expand.

Those moments really do it for me.

Debra Salazar
Age 41

The connection between all life comes full circle in the earth's water system. A single drop goes over the falls and blends and becomes one with all the drops below. Together they gather strength and beauty. Rivers run over falls into lakes and oceans, evaporating up into clouds and back down as rainfall. Without this cycle and interconnection, all life would fail.

I play my flute as a thank you to nature. It is the only thing I can give back that is uniquely my own creation. It is a private moment that cements the bond I feel with the Mother.

Kendra Dorothy Williams-Brown
Age 42

Water is the Source of All Life and Teacher of All Her Lessons

Power and Grace

I'm in my power when I'm working out: cycling, running, rowing, hiking. The rhythm of my steps or strokes is meditative and lifts me to a level that transcends thought or words. The power I feel nourishes my soul.

I take great pleasure in moving smoothly and powerfully no matter what I'm doing. I especially enjoy cycling since it naturally lends itself to fluidity and grace.

Liz Feeney
Age 33

Power is Most Becoming on Those Who Mirror It

Connecting with people and problem solving — these are my strengths. Dealing with areas which are stressful, calming people down, and analyzing basic components of situations is where I excel. When I'm with clients, co-workers, and friends, I listen, analyze and reflect upon their actions and reactions. I've been told that I give valuable feedback and offer clear-cut advice. This is because I help others to see their own power and accept, or at least acknowledge, their responsibilities. When others use me to come to these realizations, it empowers me as well.

Incomplete woman
Listens, gathers, supports ties;
Sees no end to growth.

Sandra E. Jones
Age 47

Nourishing the Body; Nourishing the Spirit

*W*hether cooking for friends or working as a professional caterer, I find that I am comfortable and centered during my time in the kitchen. This is work that I love, so it leaves me feeling happy and powerful. Because I have become secure in my ability to do this job well, I am more apt to experiment and trust my creativity.

While in college working on an English teaching degree, I took a job at a little European-style bakery. I discovered my calling and altered my course. I believe I'm a happier person today because of this decision. I now teach student workers how to bake. I absolutely love working with this population, and it feels somewhat poetic to be combining my interests in cooking and teaching.

Karina Davidson
Age 43

All my life I have felt "called" to be a volunteer. When my four daughters were young, it was with church, Girl Scouts, and PTA. Now that I have retired from teaching, I have enjoyed coordinating volunteers for Habitat for Humanity. This organization helps low-income families build homes with volunteer labor, some donated materials, and no-interest mortgages.

Dealing with college students, employed and retired people, and new homeowners, I find I am always in contact with someone interesting. It is satisfying for me to bring people and tasks together and to see their pride in contributing to an important cause.

Volunteering keeps me quite active and adds a lot of variety to my life. When someone tells me that they need my "special" talents for a specific job, I almost always say yes. That's the way it is with born volunteers.

Dorothy Buttler Angell
Age 73

Called to Volunteer

Total Drive

I can be running, when suddenly I make a transition. I realize that I want to push myself as hard as I can. To test myself to see how fast I can go. I'm not hurting, and I have the confidence that I'm going to be able to really perform that day. I'm not feeling compelled from the outside to push and perform. It's totally from within. There is such a feeling of integration within all parts of myself, and that integration is connected with everything around me. My legs respond to my command to charge up the hill. The road is propelling me forward. The hills are pulling me up the grade. The horizon is pulling me toward it. It's a wonderful state of mind. I'm feeling a passion to do well and that passion feeds my physical state and that physical state feeds my passion.

I think that this is what it means to be an athlete.

Debbie Chaddock
Age 35

The Dance of Sisterhood

"When are you in your power?" I was asked. "I'm not sure," I said. "Unless, you mean when I feel happy and creative. I feel creative when I put things together, as simple as a bouquet of fall flowers that I gathered on the roadside, or rearranging a room so that it "feels" more friendly. But mostly, I feel happy when I am working with a group of women. That connection with other women feels like an old memory which I am longing to remember and acknowledge. When this connection happens, it feels like "coming home," like being seen for who I am, and seeing other women as part of me. It goes beyond blood relation, but seems as old as time and stretches across culture, and even language. "That must be it," I said, "I feel in my power when I am in good relationship with the "sisterhood" of all women everywhere!" Two incidents where I felt this connection immediately came to mind.

The first was when I lived with my family in East Africa. We worked as volunteers in a group of community self-help projects across Kenya. We held training institutes for volunteers from every district, mostly young men and women, on ways to improve basic health, diversify farming methods, start small businesses, and engender community spirit. After working and living with these Kenyan volunteers for four years, we became like family. When Lucy and Donald Kiilu invited me and my family to visit Machakos and their home village of Kitui, of course we accepted. Their mothers and a group of village women met us as they returned from the river carrying large containers of water. They showed us around their shambas (farms) and then fed us a delicious meal of chicken, Ugali (like stiff corn mush) and Kitheri (maize and beans). Although we couldn't speak their local dialect, they treated us like extended family. Before we left, the women spontaneously formed a circle on the grassy knoll and started to dance and sing. They beckoned for me to come and join them. I followed their lead as they clapped and stomped in rhythm with each other and me. It was so much fun, this dance and laughter, — their love of life was so contagious! They laughed at my attempts to sing the words, but when our eyes met, I felt as if I had known them all my life. I felt welcomed into their circle, accepted as a woman. Although I couldn't speak their language, there in that shamba, moving to the magic of that earth-stomping dance, we connected as

Sisters. It was truly one of the happiest moments of our time there, participating in their dance and being encircled by my global sisters, the women of Kituii.

More recently, back in the States, I have been involved with a spiritual women's group. I had a dream of creating an herb garden together as a way to help us remember about plants. I am not a gardener, so I went on faith that it would happen. An afternoon was picked to start working on it. Some women brought herb seedlings, another brought a truckload of dirt and plenty of rakes. Others just came to work. Some women knew which herbs made good teas, others knew which were good to burn for their aroma. Others knew how to cook with them. By the end of the afternoon, a beautiful garden had taken shape! Each month brought new growth and beauty, and there was always an abundance of herbs to use in recipes or to arrange into a fresh bouquet. A large round rock had been placed in the center of the garden and women often went there to sit and muse on life. Often, we said our gratitude prayers in the garden, thanking the plants for their gift of life to us. Different people kept it watered and weeded and, by the end of the year, the results were spectacular! I loved learning about all the different kinds of lavender and never imagined there were so many different shades of gold, orange, and red in those simple, happy nasturtiums. I think that the success of that herb garden was that it had been created out of a sense of women community, —without competition, pettiness, or criticism. It grew because we worked in a spirit of shared responsibility and cooperation. It flourished because we loved and appreciated the plants which brought such beauty to that space and, therefore, to our group. And, it wasn't just my dream, it was OUR dream.

As we bring our dreams and stories into reality, we become mirrors to each other. My sister's story is MY story, my story is HER story. As we link arm in arm, we strengthen the circle of life through our shared human experience. Together, we make our world a better place, flourishing as we share and live in cooperation with one another, and radiating with our unique expression of courage and inner beauty.

- Maxine Norton
Age 54

I express myself aesthetically in a raw sense. It is automatic. Instinctual. Things fly. I feel like I have an inner measuring graph in my eyes that demands that things be completely balanced. When I'm working, I'm really focused and engaged. I have ideas in my head and can see a piece in my mind. I know what I have to do first. I just start doing it. When I'm through, the space is filled with the right shapes. There is balance and color where there wasn't any. And that calms me.

Annie Torgersen
Age 33

Filling Spaces

Great Mystery teaches me through the Earth Mother and all her beings, touching me in a deeply sacred, sensual and beautiful way. I am in my full power when I teach and reflect this world back to others - inviting them in to my inner lush and magical forest glen. With them, I share how my pain, hurt, and sorrow has been transformed into wisdom, grace and joy. I show them how my travels to sacred places of the earth have been transformed into stories, poetry, paintings, and objects of beauty. And I allow them to relax into my living space, which reflects the magic of light and comfort.

I remind my sisters and brothers of their own inner gardens and abilities to transform their worlds. Then I send them on their pathway with a hug.

I am grateful to all who express their power and teach me to be able to express and recognize mine.

Carol Eve
Age 53

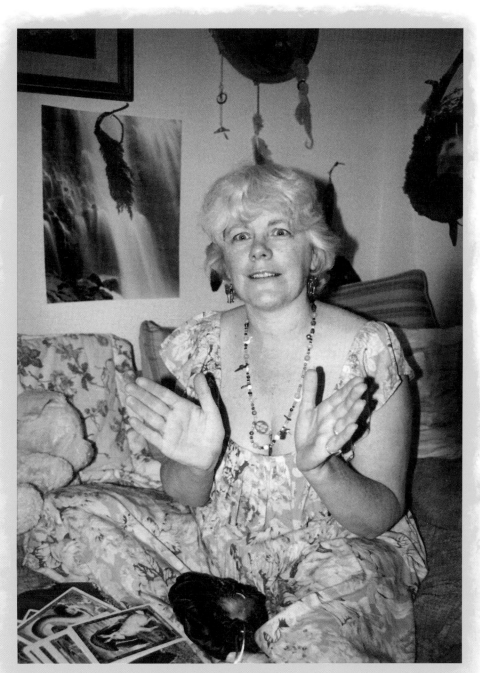

I Create an Inspiring and Comforting Sacred Space

I Teach For The World To Be More Equal

*M*y parents left the Old Country for the Gold Mountain, America, in pursuit of a better life. Period. That's what they always told me. They knew it was going to be hard work. And, if good fortune didn't immediately smile upon them, they knew it would through their children.

I am the daughter of Chinese immigrants. My parents saw education as a gold nugget from the mountain - it was the key to success and happiness. Family law mandated that I learn, and "learn to be the best."

When I was little, the outdoors was my teacher. I learned about peace and equality in the wooded lots where I lived. I ran to them when mean people followed me home with their ugliness. The trees protected me. The flowers soothed my soul. The soft brown earth absorbed my frustrations. I promised myself that I would do something to help make life more fair.

As an adult, I've found my power in environmental education. I love my job at the Aquarium because it allows me to serve a diversity of people, especially underprivileged children. When the story of the lesson is flowing through me and through the audience, I feel that I've arrived at the Gold Mountain.

Knowing is not enough; we must apply. Willing is not enough; we must do.

-Goethe

Belinda Chin
Age 35

Entering a Painting

When I begin to create a painting, I am initially overwhelmed, panicked. Eventually, I become immersed in the process, and the idea and colors start to come together. I get very excited.

I enjoy acrylics and monotypes. Textures and patterns. Thick paint. Big bold colors, vividness. Nothing soft or subtle at this point. For a while I was scared of bigness. Everything I did was tiny. Now I'm doing big paintings. Paintings that reach out and grab you.

Deb Dole
Age 37

No matter who I work with, it is important they trust that they are in a safe and comfortable space. I meet that need for them verbally or with my presence or with something in my work space that allows them to feel that safety. I can only create that vulnerability and trust for someone to the extent that I am willing to do that for myself.

I invite my clients to participate and give feedback as I work. This creates a dynamic atmosphere which allows us both to be involved and present in the moment. As my hands work the muscle, healing and change happen in this circular relationship.

Elizabeth Brown
Age 40

Circular Healing

Creative Joy

When I was seven, my older sister was taking crocheting in school. I begged Mom and Dad for a crochet needle, but they said that I was too young. I took a straight pin and some thread from my mom's sewing basket, watched my sister, then went under the bed and crocheted. When I showed my mom, she didn't believe I made it and put it away. I insisted that I wanted to learn, so my dad asked me to show them. I got a piece of thread and crocheted lace with the head of that straight pin. Dad went out and bought me a needle.

I've been teaching for the Parks Department for twenty-one years. I teach because I know a lot about crafts, and it relaxes me. I do knitting, sewing, macrame, embroidery, and ceramics. I've mostly taught seniors because it gets them out of the house and keeps them active. Sometimes they are lonesome or bored at home. I feel real proud because it is something I can give.

Idessa Nash
Age 88

After a childhood of moving many times and an adult life of buying and fixing and living in different houses, I have finally found and created a home. The process of recognizing this farm as home has meant a recognition of my own stability and serenity.

My home gives me the confidence to go out in the world, be weirdly funny, and to be happy in my career. My friends and family know they will find a safe and fun place to be; I know that I just have to look within my home and myself to find an immutable source of energy and strength.

Terri Briant Booth
Age 43

Home Is a Base of Serenity and Strength

*H*iking changes my conscious state. As I'm climbing in the mountains, thoughts extend and drift undisturbed. The wildness draws me inside where I remember to trust life and intuition.

This site is a powerful spot for me. It was where I first saw madrona trees and the San Juan Islands. I was transformed by this landscape and knew to my core that the Puget Sound would be the next setting for my life. Now, I'm here again quite unexpectedly, back at this same spot after seven years, ready to face another transition. This is a place that gives its blessing for change.

Maureen Burns
Age 43

Sensing the Sea Change

Running Through the Gate

When I was first asked to write about being in my power, my mind started dancing. I would have to talk about the importance of the context; how complex it is and that there are no easy answers. I heard myself as the teacher saying, "We must consider all of the sociocultural factors that contribute to women's loss of power at the personal, political, and economic levels. Examine how sexism and ageism are inextricably linked and how societal expectations, domination, and oppression diminish women's power. And, of course, we must see how power is defined, perceived, and synthesized for each of us in a very personal and different way. All of this is so important to understand if we are going to make changes for ourselves and others."

Well, the request was to write about what it was like when I was in my power, and there it was, the academic distancing. The first wall blocking the process of looking at my power at the personal level was firmly in place. I realize that part of my power is the ability to see the forces that oppress and diminish. It is also my passion as a teacher to bring awareness and discussion about injustice and discrimination in any form. But how is all of this actualized for me? How does it feel? As I ponder this, I hear the voice saying, "I can't write this. It won't be good enough. It can't be what she wants." And so the dance begins. I can clearly see what the dance is like for me when my spirit is not full. How I'm distracted at those times, diminished; listening to judgment and internalizing my oppression. Believing I am the bad daughter, the not good mother, or the fat woman who has no control. Believing I'm not good enough.

When I'm in my power, I don't feel judged. I am truly able to see another person, recognize our connection, and give myself and my energy without restraint. Feeling that it's okay to be me. In fact, at those times it's wonderful to be me. I'm at the peak of my creativity, my optimal place; feeling good about being where I am, who I am with, and what I am doing. It's about being present. It's the times I'm laughing and playing with a child; cooking a wonderful meal for a friend; reading *The Little Prince* to Gary in bed; listening to Scott play his beautiful music; missing John and Lorrie; playing a silly game with Lynne on a road trip; connecting with a student; taking care of my mom; reveling in a sunset; and, yes...writing this piece.

The most important part for me is recognizing the dance and knowing that I have the ability to change it and not be distracted. To have a better awareness of my feelings and to not judge myself harshly.

My friend Margie and I were talking about all of this, and she told me a story about a time when, as a young girl, she and a friend decided to play a prank. There was a rather hyper little dog that ran around its yard in circles all the time. The girls decided to open the gate and let her loose, but, when they did, she just continued to run around the yard. Margie says sometimes it's like that for her. The gate is open, but she's still running around in the yard.

So, for me, it's about not running around in the yard anymore; the gate is open, and I'm free. It's about giving myself the respect, dignity, and self-determination that I value for all humankind. It's knowing that my power is simultaneously the same as everyone else's and yet, uniquely mine.

Kathleen McCue-Swift
Age 51

Standing on the earth, I often feel moved to poetry and prayer.

I reach within to the quiet space inside
Sinking ever deeper into each sigh
Cavern walls surround me
I am led
To listen
To touch
To see
All that I am
All that I am becoming with heart in hands
I stand
Holding what is sacred
What is true
As I share this now with you
Confident in my vulnerability

Mariah Mannia
Age 31

Confident Vulnerability

Writing Is A Form of Physics; When Good, It Enlightens Us

While out driving many years ago, my small daughter asked me a question. "Why are boys called sons, and girls called daughters?" Dumfounded, I hesitated. "It's very odd", she said, "because girls are warm and golden like the sun, but boys are white and distant like the moon." After a moment of shock, I comprehended. "Would you like me to call you a sun?" I asked her. She nodded.

The power of language is wonderful. Without it, we circumnavigate only feeling and image. Without it, there is no mythology, no history. Erase the words, and memory is random.

I write because I have an immense respect and gratitude for language.

Ara Taylor
Age 43

Sharing...Natural Wisdom for Living Well

Asking myself, "when am I in my power," then pausing for a moment, my inner voice replies: "I am always in my power." When we recognize and honor ourselves as spiritual beings - that means being in our power.

As we intuitively seek our balance, our paths connect us to each other in a quest for healing...physically, mentally, emotionally, and spiritually.

Healing doesn't mean that everything is perfect - it just means we feel connected and whole. This is happening with people in different cultures. We're all re-connecting with our true spiritual natures to ensure a future for our world and peace of mind for ourselves.

Lani Steagall
Age 56

I love rock. I feel really in my power when I'm climbing and my body is performing. The situation forces me to be totally present. I can't be worrying about past or future problems when I'm hanging off one edge of a cliff!

I love to be in high places. The 14th Dali Lama says, "people need to climb the mountain, not simply because it is there, but because the soul, which is at home in the deep shadowed valleys, needs to be mated with spirit."

I love being on the edge.

Mary Schultz
Age 35

Dancing on Rock

I am a nurse-practitioner in a women's health clinic. I strive to create a comforting, healing environment and make sure that I completely understand a woman's needs for that day. It is a truly powerful time when I can say, "this is what you have causing your problem, and this medicine or treatment will help to heal you."

I like to show each woman how powerful it is that her cells can tell me a story about her body. I'm looking at disease, which may not appeal to a lot of people, but if you have one, you want someone to look at it.

Kim Abbey
Age 47

The Cells Speak to Me of Another World and I Understand

*B*eing in the woods is powerful for me. The quietness of the forest gives me a feeling of deep calm. I like taking a deep breath all of the way in and smelling the cedars. Not many trees smell that good. The branches feel like a cascade of water coming down my shoulder, and all of the elements - earth, air, water, fire of the sun - are right there. It makes me feel like I'm a part of the earth. I'm within it, not upon it.

Kathie Kirsch
Age 43

Red Cedar Woman

I feel very sure of myself in my boat. I can kayak all day long, for miles and miles, with grebes and seals and cormorants for company. The first time I ever kayaked, I paddled alone on a bay in Alaska. I've loved kayaking ever since. I can paddle backwards and forwards. I surf in the waves. I am strong.

I feel very fortunate that my mom raised me to not be afraid. Sometimes she thinks she did too good a job - I don't think so. I grew up feeling I had a right to be here and that I could do anything I wanted. I didn't grow up with the notion that I shouldn't be powerful. I love to feel the power in my stroke, the force of movement in my body.

I am planning a journey - the "Girls Just Wanna Have Fun" expedition - to celebrate women in the sport of extreme sea kayaking, and the idea that the purpose of life is joy.

Nancy Rager
Age 39

Yes You Can

I have created a world that has helped me to be an empowered woman. I've started a business that I'm proud of and have drawn people into my life who have helped me to be who I am. I've learned ancient techniques from a spiritual teacher that have been modernized and made more effective for the times. They've helped me to meet people and commune with spirit. All religions are pretty much the same in how they speak about love. This has been the truth of my journey.

Victoria Schenz
Age 45

Sitting at Sunset

Acknowledgments

I would like to start by acknowledging that wonderful circle of women in Seattle who enthusiastically listened to my idea and kept their faith that I would begin when the time was right. I would also like to thank my supportive mother who, ever so gently, suggested that I might expand my exhibit idea into a book. Thank you to my sister, Cindy, who called me from Chicago every few weeks with encouragement and brainstorms. Thank you to my other sisters who cheered me on.

I am indebted to all of the women who honored me, as well as themselves, by being photographed or writing an essay - you are an inspiration to us all. I thank Starfeather for her eloquent foreword and for being an inspiring teacher. Thank you to Pam for being a coach and an anchor. I am grateful to my friends - especially, Deb, Mary, and Teresa - who happened to be there when I needed feedback and another point of view. Thank you to Terri for your fresh set of eyes. Thank you to Bob and Rupali for weaving your art over the cover and through these pages. And, most of all, thank you to Liz for supplying me with a steady stream of love, support, and laughter through every step of this project.

The following individuals appeared with participants:
Donna Cooper with Dorothy B. Angell
Emily Booth with Terri Briant Booth
Barb Richey with Elizabeth Brown
Nancy Ishii with Rashida G. Harris
Clancy McDermott with Joan Nourse Martin
Jim Hossack with Nancy Parsley
Leonne Soth with Felicia Soth
Hilde Boone with Lani Steagall

Thank you for your participation.

While this book was in progress, Belinda Chin lost her father and Nancy Rager her mother. I would like to acknowledge these parents and honor them for raising such wonderful daughters.

Comments

Thank you, participants, for all of your positive feedback. Here are some of your comments:

This whole process has been a wonderful gift...thanks for including me.

As shy as I am about pictures of myself, there were actually quite a few I really liked. I'm excited to see how the whole thing turns out!

I want to thank you. I want to thank you. I want to thank you. This is not a casual thank you. When we finished our conversation, I felt absolutely quieted and could barely say another word. I just wanted to give you a hug. Your questions moved me to the next step.

To be approached and have someone take an interest in what I'm doing felt like the icing on my cake of 62 candles.

I always knew what I loved doing, but going through this process really raised my awareness. I can now recognize those times when I'm in my power.

This was so much fun!

I wish everyone could go through this interview process - it was so powerful. It is such a gift to spend time focusing on such a positive aspect of oneself; I felt so unexpectedly honored, and I don't imagine I would have ever done it for myself.

Every morning when I wake up, I look at my picture, and it reminds me of how I'm useful in this world.

Index

Traveling Exhibit

My Spirit Flies: Portraits and Prose of Women In Their Power

Several of the portraits in this book have been used
to create a traveling exhibit. If you are interested in
finding out how to bring this exhibit to your area,
please contact Cathy Angell at:

Bay City Press
P.O. Box 1213
Bellingham, WA 98227

(360) 714-1982
(360) 714-1673 (fax)

Ordering Information

My Spirit Flies: Portraits and Prose of Women In Their Power
By M. Cathy Angell / 96 pages / $24.95

Personal Empowerment Questionnaire (Discover *Your* Power)
By M. Cathy Angell / $3.00

Price List of Black and White Custom Prints from *My Spirit Flies*
By M. Cathy Angell

Postal Orders: **Bay City Press**
                     Box 1213
                     Bellingham, WA 98227

Phone Orders: (360) 714-1982
Fax Orders: (360) 714-1673
On-Line Orders: cangell2@aol.com

Shipping: $4.00 for first book; $2.00 for each additional book.
WA State residents add 8.2% Sales Tax

Photographer M. Cathy Angell has been capturing people on film since the early 1980's. Her work has been purchased by the City of Seattle's 1% for Art program, displayed at KCTS Channel 9, and published in *Family Circle* Magazine. It has also appeared on the covers of annual reports and featured in publicity campaigns for government and non-profit agencies.

Cathy seemed destined to work with women. At the age of eight she attended Girl Scout camp and became imprinted with the image of confident women who had outdoor skills, strong singing voices, a love of the earth, and an understanding of sisterhood. She saw the possibilities. These influences carried her to adulthood where she has sat in circle with women for several years - listening to their stories, singing, and growing together. Through her experiences, she has witnessed firsthand the transformation that takes place when women pay attention to those things which feed their souls.

She lives with her partner in Bellingham, Washington, where she continues to photograph and help women shift their vision and acknowledge their inner power.